The World OF INSECTS

EVERYDAY INSECTS

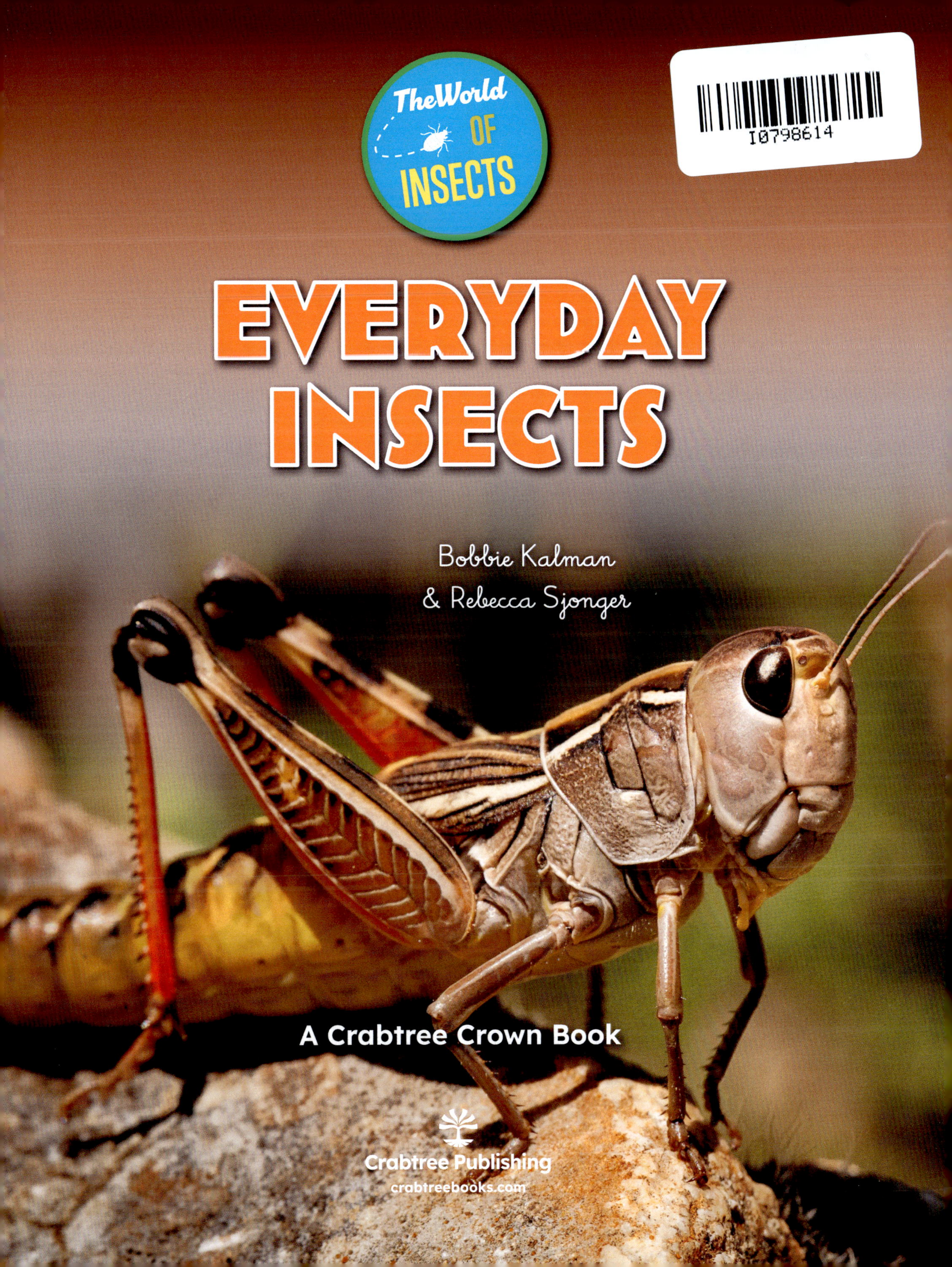

Bobbie Kalman
& Rebecca Sjonger

A Crabtree Crown Book

Crabtree Publishing
crabtreebooks.com

EVERYDAY INSECTS

Editor-in-Chief Bobbie Kalman

Writing team Bobbie Kalman, Rebecca Sjonger

Editors Kathryn Smithyman, Molly Aloian, Robin Johnson, Kristina Lundblad, Kelley MacAulay

Consultant Patricia Loesche, Ph.D., Animal Behavior Program, Department of Psychology, University of Washington

Design and photo research Katherine Kantor

Cover design Rhea Magaro-Wallace

Production manager Candice Campbell

Images Shutterstock

Crabtree Publishing

crabtreebooks.com 800-387-7650

In Canada: We acknowledge the financial support of the Government of Canada through the Canada Book Fund for our publishing activities.

Printed in the U.S.A./CP022026

Published in Canada
Crabtree Publishing
616 Welland Ave.
St. Catharines, Ontario
L2M 5V6

Published in the United States
Crabtree Publishing
347 Fifth Ave
Suite 1402-145
New York, NY 10016

Library and Archives Canada Cataloguing in Publication
Available at the Library and Archives Canada

Library of Congress Cataloging-in-Publication Data
Available at the Library of Congress

Hardcover: 978-1-0398-7304-9
Paperback: 978-1-0398-7362-9
Ebook (pdf): 978-1-0398-7412-1
Epub: 978-1-0398-7461-9

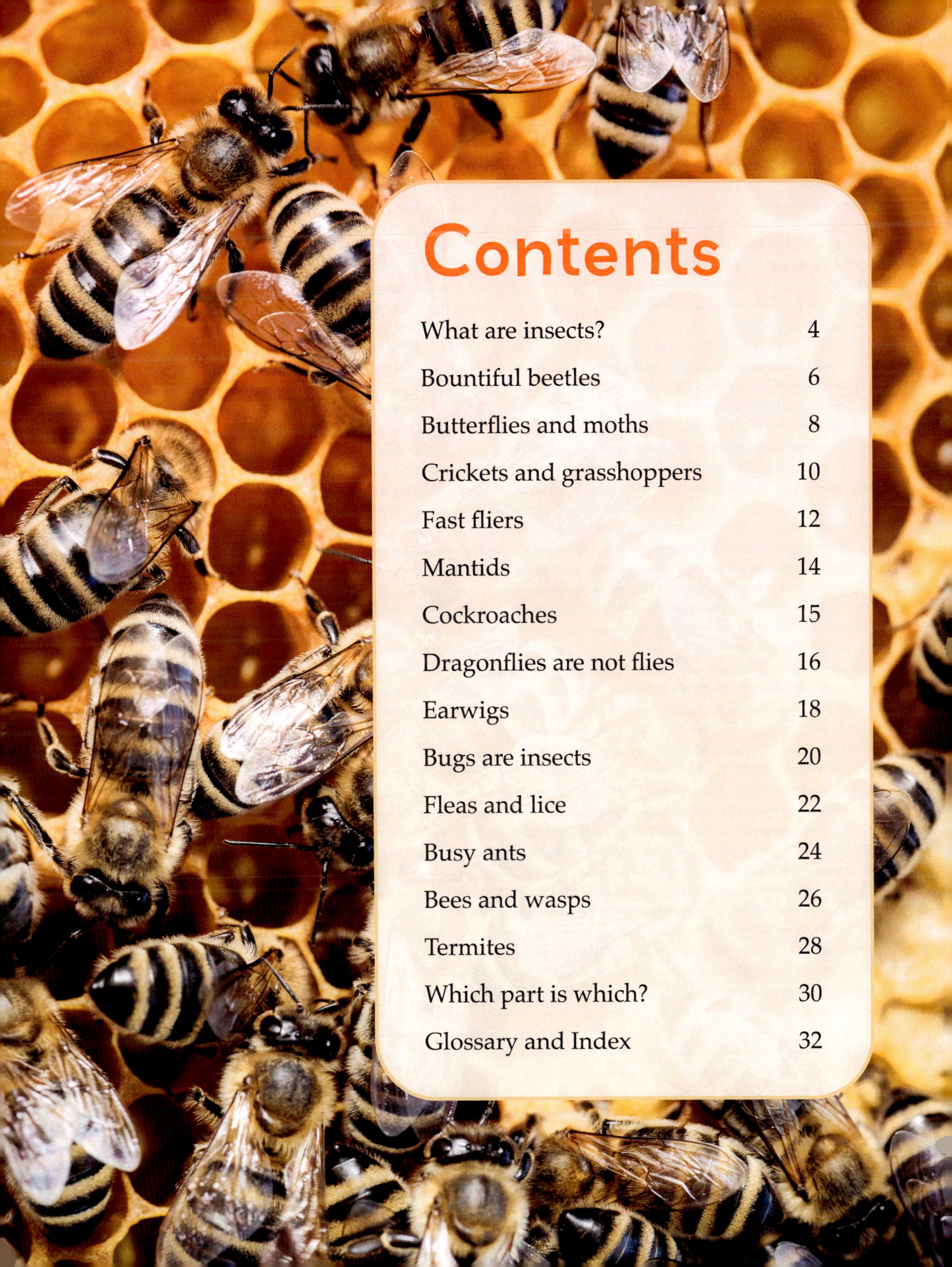

Contents

What are insects?

Insects are animals called **invertebrates**. An invertebrate does not have a **backbone**. A backbone is a group of bones in the middle of an animal's back. Instead of a backbone, an insect has an **exoskeleton**. An exoskeleton is a hard covering that protects an insect's body.

Everyday insects

This book is about **everyday insects**, or insects that are common in many parts of the world. Ants, flies, beetles, and termites are just a few of the insects that people know or see often. These insects may be found in forests, fields, gardens, yards, and even inside homes!

This cricket's exoskeleton covers its whole body, including its head and legs.

Insect bodies

An insect's body has three main sections—a head, a **thorax**, and an **abdomen**. On its head, the insect has eyes, **mouthparts**, and two feelers called **antennae**. It has six legs attached to its thorax. Some insects also have wings on their thoraxes. The insect's abdomen is the back section of its body.

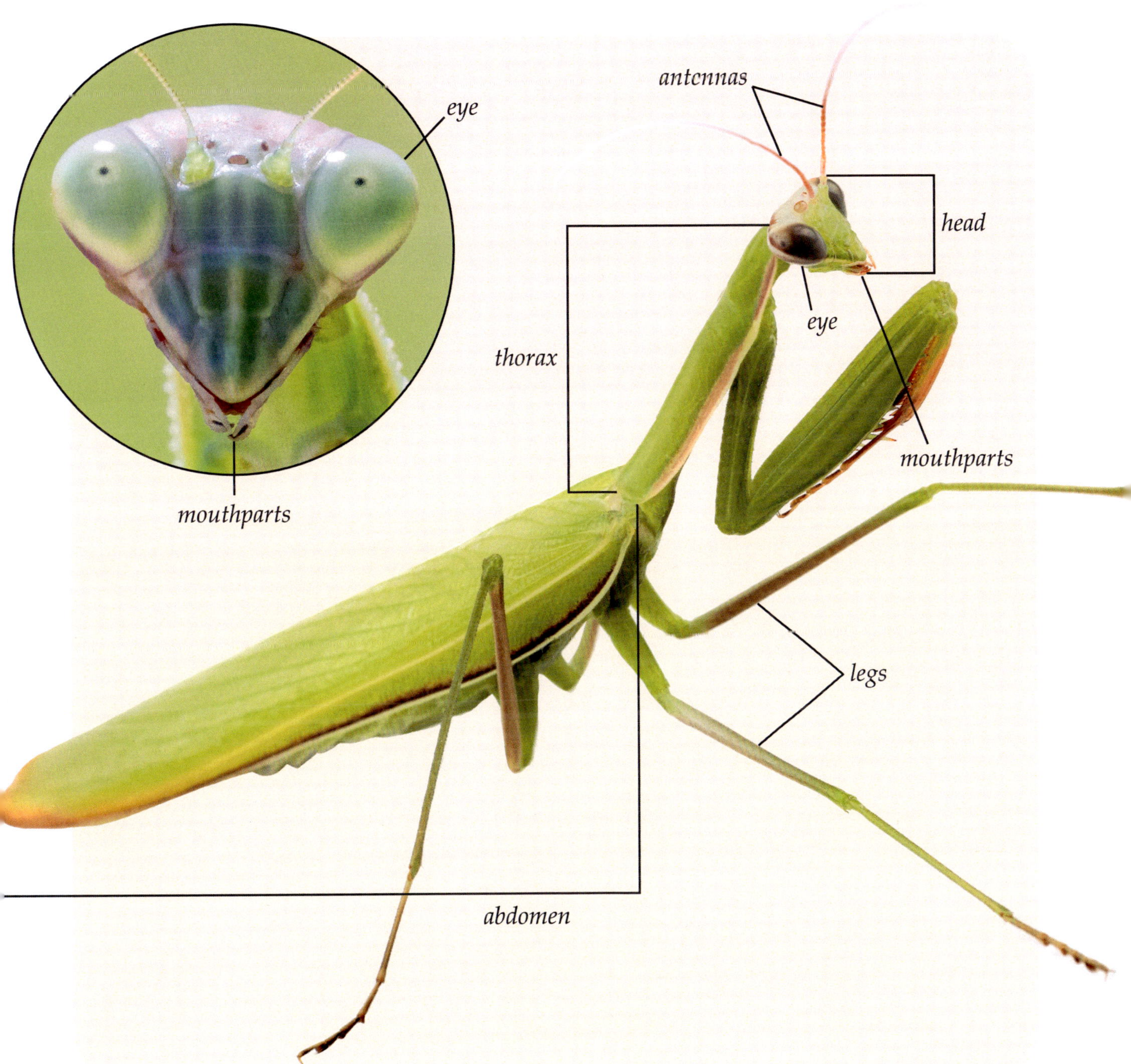

Bountiful beetles

There are over 350,000 known **species**, or types, of beetles. Species that are similar to one another are grouped together. Fireflies, tiger beetles, and weevils are three groups of beetles.

Beetle homes

Some beetles, such as leaf beetles, live on trees and other plants. Other beetles, such as the ground beetle shown below, live under logs, stones, and dead leaves. Beetles also live in grassy areas. Water beetles live near, on, or in lakes, rivers, ponds, and other bodies of water.

Ladybugs are beetles that often live in people's yards or gardens.

Nature's helpers

Many everyday insects, including beetles, help keep the environment healthy. Insect **scavengers** eat dead or dying plants and animals. Burying beetles are scavengers. Other beetles, including ladybugs, are **carnivores**. Carnivores are animals that eat other animals. Ladybugs eat plant-destroying insects such as aphids.

When ladybugs eat aphids, farmers and gardeners can grow certain plants without using harmful ***pesticides****.*

A burying beetle uses its sharp jaws to bite into its food. Its jaws are called ***mandibles****.*

Butterflies and moths

Butterflies and moths are known for their big, beautiful wings. People can often tell butterflies and moths apart by looking at their wings. Most butterflies have brightly colored wings, whereas most moths have dull-colored wings. There are about 17,500 species of butterflies and about 160,000 species of moths.

When a butterfly rests on a flower or other surface, it holds its wings straight up in the air, as shown above.

Sweet treats

Many species of butterflies and moths drink **nectar**. Nectar is a sweet liquid found in flowers. In a garden or field, you may see a butterfly flying from flower to flower to drink nectar.

Did you know?

Most butterfly and moth species are active at different times of the day. Butterflies are usually active during the day. They rest at night. Moths are often active after dark. They rest during the day.

Notice how a moth holds its wings when it is resting. When a moth rests, it brings its wings down to cover its body.

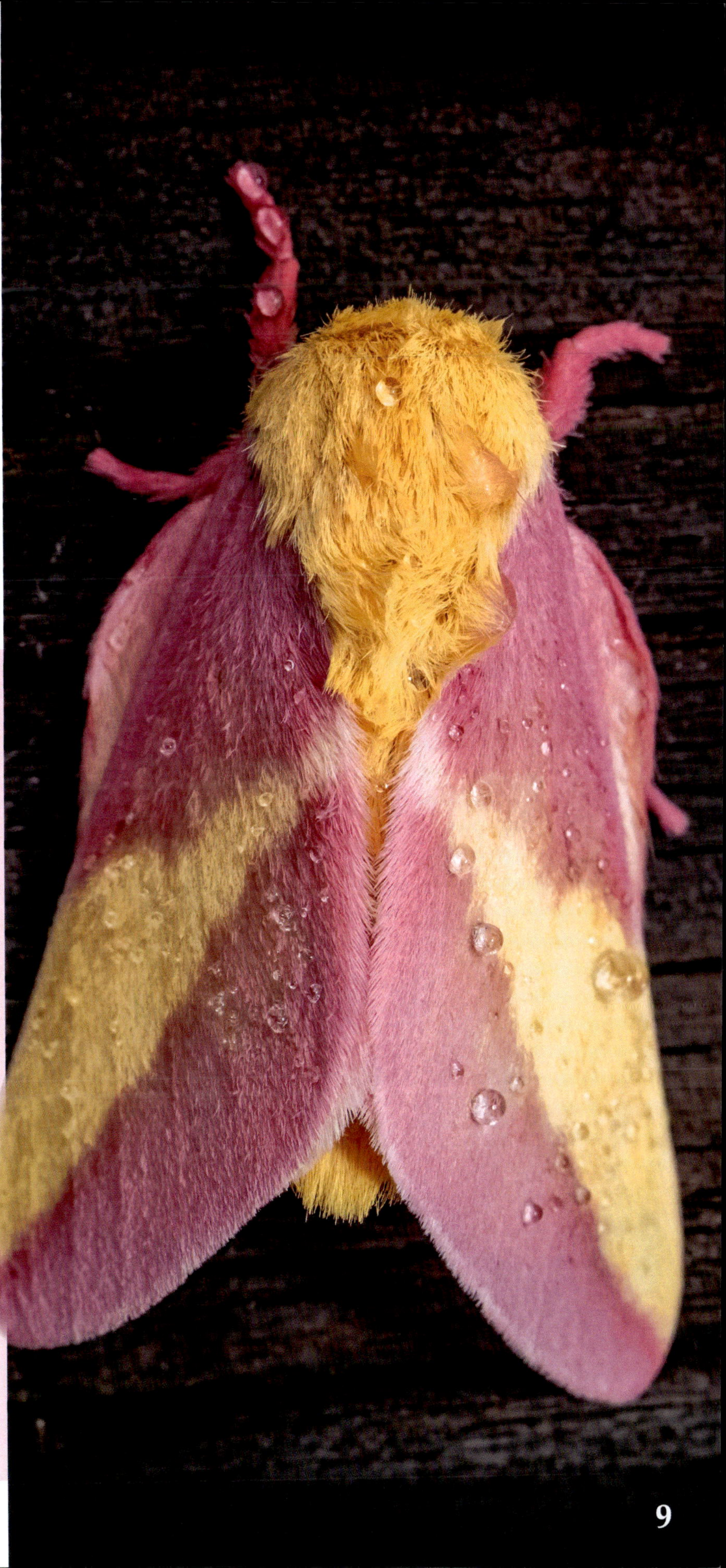

Crickets and grasshoppers

Crickets and grasshoppers are great jumpers! They use their strong back legs to jump from place to place. Crickets and grasshoppers can jump away quickly from hungry **predators**. Predators are animals that hunt and eat other animals. Most grasshoppers can also fly to safety, but crickets rarely fly.

Masters of disguise

When crickets and grasshoppers are not moving, they can be hard to see! Like most insects, many crickets and grasshoppers have **camouflage**. Camouflage is colors, textures, or patterns on an animal's body that help hide the animal in the natural place where it lives.

Some grasshoppers have camouflage, which helps them blend in with the plants or the ground on which they live.

Crickets and grasshoppers do not use their two pairs of front legs while jumping.

Chirp!

Crickets and grasshoppers make chirping sounds with their bodies. Male crickets and grasshoppers often chirp to attract female partners. Some of these insects chirp by rubbing together the **veins** at the bottom of their front wings. Others chirp by rubbing the veins of their front wings along their back legs.

Did you know?

The chirps of some male crickets are very loud! Male mole crickets, such as the one shown above, chirp loudly. They live under the ground in tunnels. To attract female mole crickets, males chirp from inside their tunnels.

Fast fliers

House flies, fruit flies, horse flies, and mosquitoes are some of the different kinds of flies found almost everywhere. As the name "fly" suggests, flies are great at flying! House flies, such as the one shown below, are excellent flyers because they can beat their wings very quickly.

Buzz off!

Have you ever heard a fly "buzz" as it whizzes through the air? The sound comes from the fly's wings. A fly's wings flap so quickly that air rushes around them, creating a buzzing sound. Bees and dragonflies also make buzzing sounds when they fly.

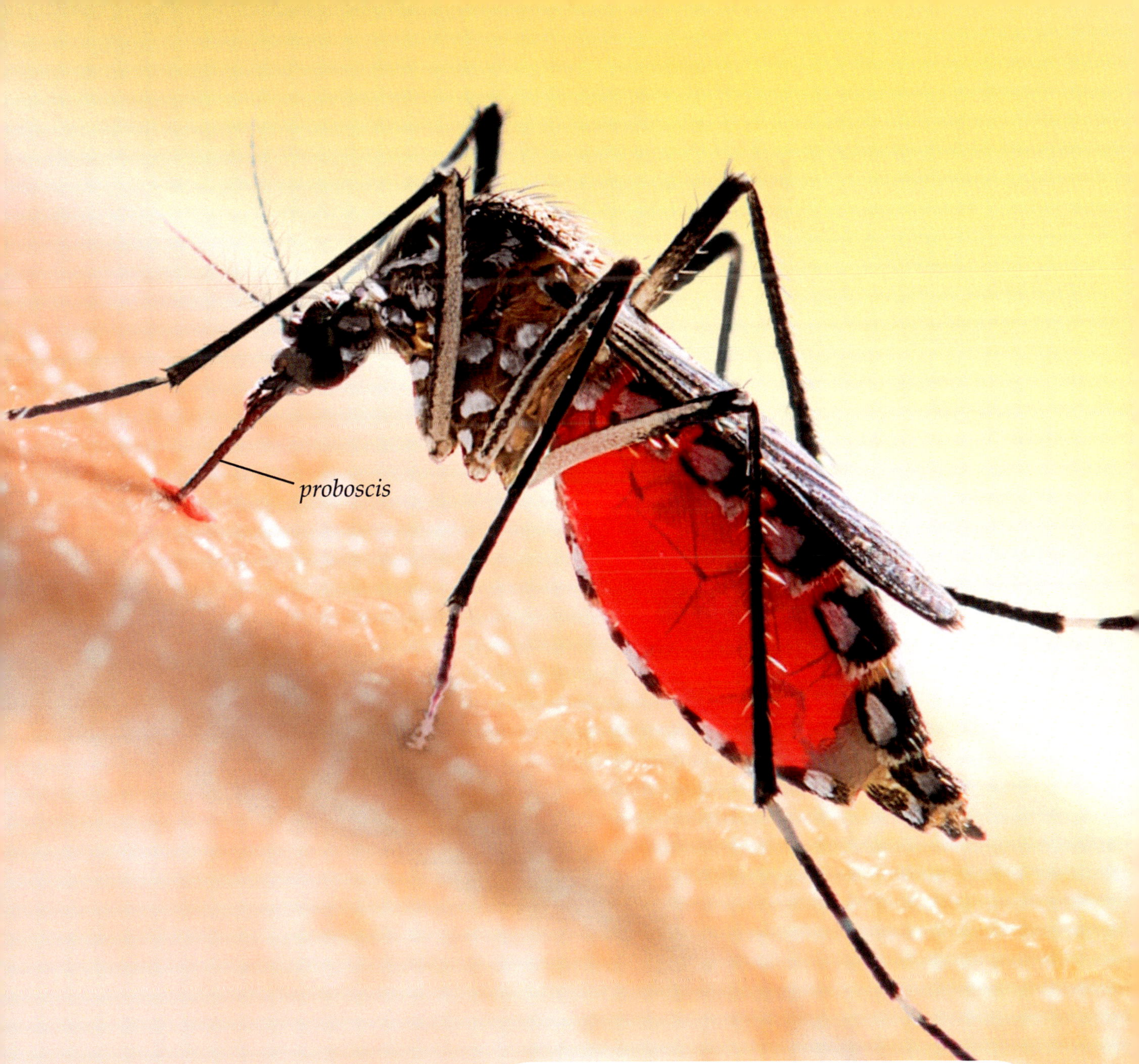

Chow down

A fly uses its sensitive antennae and large eyes to find food. Different species of flies eat different foods. Some flies drink nectar. Other flies eat dead animals or animal waste. Some even drink blood!

Did you know?

A female mosquito, shown above, drinks blood. To drink blood, the mosquito uses a long, thin mouthpart called a **proboscis**. The mosquito sticks its proboscis into an animal's skin. It then sucks up the animal's blood through the proboscis.

Mantids

Mantids are often known as "praying mantises." While resting, a mantid folds its front legs together in front of its head. In this position, a mantid looks like it is praying. It is actually "preying," or waiting for **prey**. Prey are the animals it hunts.

Gotcha!

Mantids sit very still when prey such as flies are nearby. When a fly is within reach, a mantid quickly stretches out its strong front legs. It uses the large hooked parts at the end of its legs to grab and hold the fly. The mantid then eats the fly.

This mantid is using the hooks at the end of its legs to hold on to the fly it is eating.

This mantid is waiting on the stem of a flower to catch prey.

Cockroaches

Many cockroach species live in trees or in underground tunnels called **burrows**. Some cockroaches live in people's houses or apartments, however! Species such as German cockroaches are attracted to people's warm, cozy homes. These insects can squeeze their slim bodies into drains or tight spaces such as under floorboards.

During the day, cockroaches rest in hiding spots. At night, they move into the open and search for food. Cockroaches will eat anything from human food to leather shoes to books!

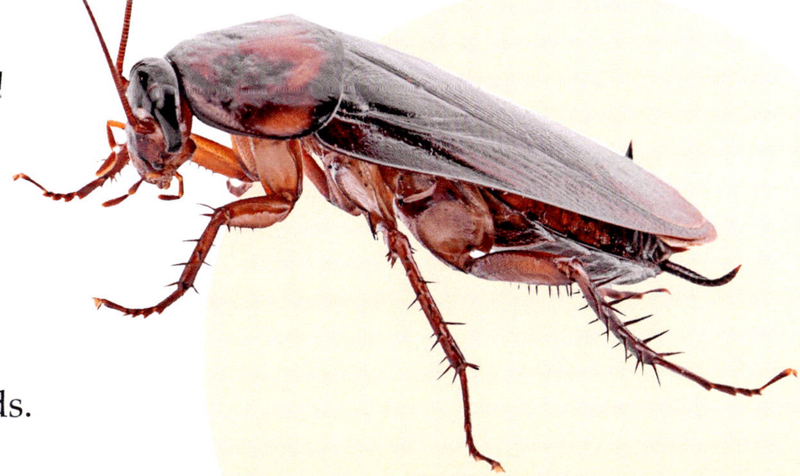

Dragonflies are not flies

Dragonflies are not really flies. Like flies, however, dragonflies are skilled fliers. Dragonflies have two pairs of long wings, which they use to fly quickly from place to place. Even birds find it difficult to catch dragonflies!

Super sight

Dragonflies can see well. Like almost all insects, dragonflies have two **compound eyes**. Compound eyes are made up of many tiny parts called **facets**. A dragonfly's compound eyes are so large that they cover most of its head! Having large, round eyes helps the insect see all around its body.

A dragonfly's compound eyes are so big that they almost touch each other!

Carnivores

Like many other insects, including mantids and some beetles, dragonflies are carnivores. They have sharp, powerful mouthparts for biting into prey such as house flies and even other dragonflies!

Did you know?

Dragonflies are closely related to damselflies. These insects look similar. The bodies of damselflies are usually more **fragile** than the bodies of dragonflies. Damselflies do not fly as well as dragonflies do.

damselfly

A dragonfly uses its good eyesight and excellent flying skills to catch prey. It spots its prey in midair and swoops in to grab the insect. The dragonfly eats its meal while still in the air.

Earwigs

Most earwig species are **nocturnal**. Nocturnal insects sleep during the day and are active at night. During the day, earwigs rest under rocks or under leaves on the ground. Once it is dark, earwigs come out of their hiding places to search for food.

Finding food

Many earwigs are **omnivores**. Omnivores are animals that eat both plants and other animals. Some earwigs eat plants such as flowers. They also eat small insects such as aphids. Other earwigs are scavengers.

Earwigs have two sharp ***pincers*** *that they use to defend themselves against other animals.*

Earwig mothers

After a mother earwig lays her eggs, she guards them until young earwigs hatch. She feeds and protects the young earwigs. Once the earwigs begin to grow, they must leave their mother, however. Otherwise, she may attack and even eat her own young!

Did you know?

Earwigs are called "earwigs" because people once believed that these insects crawled into human ears or pinched ears with their pincers! Earwigs do not usually crawl into people's ears, and they use their pincers to defend themselves from other animals.

A mother earwig lays up to 50 eggs at a time! She finds a safe spot in which to lay her eggs. The spot may be hidden beneath a log or under the ground.

Bugs are insects

All bugs are insects, but not all insects are bugs! Bugs make up an insect group that includes about 67,500 species. Every bug has a body part called a **rostrum**. A rostrum is a long, narrow tube attached to a bug's head. The bug uses its rostrum like a straw to suck up liquids such as nectar.

Bug food

Although many bugs eat plants, some bugs are predators that hunt for prey. They use their rostrums to suck the liquids out of the bodies of their prey.

A hungry bug stabs its sharp rostrum into the body of its prey. The bug then forces its ***saliva****, or spit, into the prey. The saliva makes the other insect unable to move. The bug then sucks out its prey's insides!*

Stinky bugs!

Most bugs have body parts that produce liquids that smell horrible! When a predator attacks one of these bugs, the bug makes a stink that is so terrible that it drives away the attacker. The predator will probably avoid that type of bug the next time it is hungry!

Did you know?

Insect names can be confusing! Not all insects that people call "bugs" are actually bugs. June bugs, for example, are beetles. Other insects such as water striders are bugs, even though the word "bug" is not in their names.

Fleas and lice

Fleas are **parasites**. Parasites are animals that live on the skin or in the bodies of other animals, which are called **hosts**. Fleas live in the fur, feathers, or hair of hosts such as dogs, chickens, and humans.

Feasting fleas

Fleas use sharp **stylets** to feed on the blood of their hosts. Stylets are mouthparts that can cut into an animal's flesh. A flea uses its stylets to bite into its host and suck up its blood. The bites may cause itching or pain to the hosts.

Fleas jump to move from host to host. This flea has jumped onto a person's skin.

Parasitic lice cannot jump or fly. They crawl from one host to another.

Parasitic lice

Some lice are also parasites. About 5,500 species of lice make up a group of lice called **parasitic lice**. These lice live and feed on host animals. In addition to blood, parasitic lice eat hair, flakes of skin, and even the dead bodies of other lice. Head lice are a common species of parasitic lice. As their name suggests, head lice live on people's heads!

Did you know?

Adult head lice use tiny, hooked claws to hold on to human hairs. The lice also lay sticky **nits**, or eggs, in hair. The eggs are hard to remove! People must use special shampoos and combs to remove the lice and the eggs from their hair.

Busy ants

Ants are common **social insects**. Social insects live together in large groups called **colonies**. The ants in a colony survive by working together. Every ant in a colony performs certain duties. The duties include building the home, finding food, raising young ants, and protecting the colony from predators.

Queen ants have much larger bodies than worker ants have.

Important roles

Most of the ants in a colony are **workers**. Workers carry out all the daily activities for the colony. Some worker ants are called **soldiers**. Soldier ants defend the colony from predators. Most ant colonies also have one female ant who is the **queen**. The queen is the only ant in the colony that lays eggs.

Ant nests

An ant colony lives in a home called a **nest**. Many ant species build nests in soil. Worker ants make the nest by digging tunnels in the soil. The tunnels house all the ants in the colony. Some species of ants use leaves or rotting wood to build nests.

Carpenter ant nests are often found in and around rotting wood.

Bees and wasps

Bees and wasps are everyday insects that sting. Stinging insects have **stingers**, or needlelike body parts, on the tips of their abdomens. The stingers contain **venom**, or poison.

Social and solitary

Some species of bees and wasps are social insects. Honeybees and bumblebees are social bees. Yellow jackets and hornets are social wasps. Colonies of these bees and wasps live in nests called **hives**. Other species of bees and wasps are **solitary insects**. Solitary insects live alone. Solitary bees and wasps live alone in nests.

Many species of bees and wasps have yellow-and-black striped bodies. The stripes warn predators that bees and wasps may sting to protect themselves.

Herbivores and omnivores

Bees are **herbivores**. Herbivores eat only plant foods. Like many other insects, bees drink a lot of nectar. Some bees also eat **pollen**. Wasps are omnivores. In addition to nectar, yellow jackets and other wasps eat fruit. Some wasps, such as ichneumon wasps, also eat other insects.

This bumblebee is using its proboscis to drink nectar from a flower. Its body is covered in pollen from the flower.

This wasp has caught an insect to eat and has brought it to its nest.

Termites

Termites are social insects that live in large colonies. There may be millions of termites in a single colony! Termite colonies are often found in or near wood, such as trees and **lumber**.

Many termite species chew and eat wood. As they eat the wood, they make tunnels and **chambers**, or rooms. A termite colony lives together in the tunnels and chambers.

Protecting the colony

Termite colonies include workers and soldiers. Termite soldiers are fierce insects! They protect their colonies from predators such as ants. Termite soldiers have large bodies and mandibles, which they use to fight off predators.

Termite soldiers must often defend their colonies against ants.

Did you know?

Each termite colony has only one female and one male that can **mate**, or join together to make babies. These termites are the colony's queen and king.

A termite queen can produce between 2,000 and 3,000 eggs each day!

Which part is which?

Many of the everyday insects in this book have body parts that help them move, eat, and defend themselves. Match the insects on this page with the body parts shown on page 31. If you need help, look back through the book to find the answers!

This insect uses its proboscis to take a sweet drink.

This insect uses its wings to fly high in the sky.

This insect uses its compound eyes to see all around its body.

Have no fear! This insect will not pinch you with its pincers.

Glossary

Note: Boldfaced words that are defined in the text may not appear in the glossary.

colony A group of the same kind of animals that live closely together

fragile Describing something that is weak or delicate, which can be easily broken or damaged

lumber Wood that has been cut and made into boards

pesticide A chemical that people use to kill insects

pollen A yellow, powdery substance that is found in flowers

proboscis A long, thin, tubelike mouthpart that certain insects, such as mosquitoes and honeybees, use to drink

vein A hard body part that supports an insect's wing

Index